INHALE

EXHALE

cover and book design:
Scrying Tikis carved by Charles Wehrenberg
interior rice-paper design texture
Poppies Listening by Sally Larsen
on the road 35 mm slide portrait
Charles Wehrenberg 1967 by Ed Bear

ISBN 978 1-886163-21 8

first SZP POD edition

Ceci n'est pas une pipe

Neeli's muse
emoji connotes a conversation
with a rare backyard bard
and friend of 50 years

in memoriam

Neeli Cherkovski
1945 - 2024

see page 313 - 340

IN ONE BREATH

Charles Wehrenberg

Solo Zone Publishing
San Francisco

also by Charles Wehrenberg

The Money Tree *a marijuana grow book* offered privately as hand-typed copies -- 1968

Games of Competitive Relaxation bio-input table game: *Will Ball* -- 1973/75

Deep Relaxation, the Meditative Control of Smoking & Overeating LP -- 1975

Channel 1 Mood Synthesizer booklet -- *1980*

Channel 1 Mood Synthesizer patent -- *1982*

Round Bottom Volumetric patent -- *1982*

A Private Passion fine art article *UNITED Inflight Magazine* -- April 1984

Will Ball, the Game of Competitive Relaxation, software for Apple II -- 1984

An Interactive Novelist's Wish List article *New Media Magazine* -- Feb 1993

Will Ball sci-fi novel -- SZP 1995/2023

Before New York historical novel -- SZP 1995/2023

The Ploy of Cooking novel -- SZP 1995/2023

Radio-Reactive Apples stories -- SZP 1995/2023

Thrasher novel -- SZP 1998/2023

Mississippi Blue fine photography monograph -- Twin Palms 2002

Movies Worth Watching More Than Once lifestyle guide -- SZP 2005

How To Survive Your Mouth lifestyle -- SZP ebook 2010

Feng Shui with Sally Larsen, our lifestyle as a graphic novel -- SZP POD 1998/2023

Presumed Jewish - a drive through the Middle East, memoir -- SZP POD 1973/2023

Oh Say Can You See...in old photographs - 19th century US history --SZP POD 2024

Charles Wehrenberg (b.1944) in 1967 en route to San Francisco from Aspen to become an expressive contributor as a rogue scientist with an affection for fast motorcycles, creative writing and contemporary art/design. Still surfing rainbows after nearly 1000 full Moons...

for

Lady Murasaki Shikibu

Seami Motokiyo

Sen no Rikyu

and

Donald Keene

Haiku is a Japanese poetry form encapsulating zen and other Asian philosophies; each poem is the song of a nightingale and the light of the Moon. Employing careful craft, haiku poets explore what a few well-chosen words can accomplish by juxtaposing the seasonal nature of existence with the enigmas of life itself. It is held that haiku refines WAKA poetry with its 5/7/5/7/7 [beat : syllable] pattern, which is said to take root in the ground of the mind and blossom in the forest of words. This form evolved long ago to accommodate the composite voice of phonetic Japanese and pictographic Chinese writing. A great way to appreciate haiku is to get a feel for how the Japanese have used haiku in other expressive forms. These carefully-paced *spontaneous articulations* are bridges in classic Noh dramas. *Keenly observed never imagined*, this truth is also the essence of the *Japanese I-Novel*.

In my estimation, a haiku poem is what you can do with one breath...or a last gasp.

Intentional sleight of hand, these seventeen-syllable [5/7/5] wordplays zig-zag to achieve a mnemonic arc. A train of thought switches to an unanticipated track, the flow of heart encounters a mirror: *Aha! I see!* Nothing is explained, yet something of the sublime is magically revealed in one breath. Each can become a fresh way to see, think, feel, or be...if the mind is open to epiphany.

Helter-skelter heterogenous societies like our American slurry lack the tapestry of shared, nature-based emblems intrinsic to Japanese perception; while Euro-American languages lack *aizuchi*. Along with a flash title, ordinary marks like – ... ¿ ? ! can set the stage for each *Aha! moment*. Like *kireji* in Japanese, these impact how a flowing line is seen: Eyes follow flow; eyes read shape; mind associates imagery. These strophes become the hidden drum jars under a NOH dancer's foot.

The stickiness of the 5/7/5 rhythm pattern distilled from haiku as a mnemonic device fascinates me as a literary tool. I employ this essence of haiku to empower my recent *cell phone era prose*, developed over the years on ten thousand yellow **Post-it** notes! Once you have loaded this way of thinking into your mind, luminous fragments will come back to you just the right moment.

We They
Our man in the Moon
their rabbit pounding mochi
Shiso bubble gum

Interstellar

    Moon always watching

    drink water breathe air eat food

    Clouds silver and gold

Sega

Seventeenth year of
cat so weary of seeing
Pop top tuna can

Prometheus

Humans play with fire
smoldering moss, twigs, sticks, logs
Dogs gather in awe

Children

One Two Three Four Five
little fingers weaving rugs
Eating rice today

Nihonga
A nice sitting stone
hosting neither gods nor guns.
Irises in bloom

Beyond

Money loves itself
Los Angeles sprawl wallows
Beyond garden walls

Urbanites

Earthly perfections
finely wrought lines on paper
Whiskey, wine and beer

Bananas

Basho knew the game
only bananas are free
Ink doesn't write on air

Carbon Dioxide

You cannot burn more
simply because you have more.
Compound interest

Compound Interest

You cannot burn more
simply because you have more.
Carbon dioxide

More

We cannot burn more
simply because we have more.
Bugs making methane

In Fact

    You cannot take more
and ever give back enough.
Salton Sea swim suits

Snoring
    Redwoods, palms, people
    a musical score of wires
    Myriad fatties

Hangover

Dog shit in plastic
pollen, wheels, everywhere
Panhandle tai chi

Ugh!

Coalinga WOW!
hindu hell on planet Earth
Dung beetle heaven

Oblivion

Cerulean sky
bright above gray, gold below
Trails to the Northwest

Bloodlines

Peyote woman
big hair, white water, white light
California

Hollywood '74

    Chateau Marmont sprint
    by Whisky Roxy Lookout
    Long walk to Vine...Schwabs

Morning Tea
    Small spring butterfly
    white over green fluttering
    Camellia leaves

Montara Beach

That moment of glide
before you get up and go
Blue green over sand

Amerika

Wilhelm von Humboldt

Alexander von Humboldt

Humboldt County green

Tinkering '68
    Emerging from smoke
    saffron colchicine and lust
    A new kind of weed

Martha

Passenger pigeons
once dark clouds, now dead silence.
Ringneck pheasants run

History

Yore tunes oft retold
those who would write themselves in
Thin ice, dark water

Basho

The tendrils grow fast
the flowers come and go fast
The old frog watching

Heaven and Hell
    Turkeys on the run
the cat waiting patiently
Thanksgiving again

POP!

Monkey man today
yesterday's news tomorrow
Pink cotton candy

Revelations

Sun bright cactus spines
green tea steaming in a glass
Four Horsemen nearby

Dating
　　　The new same old nude
　　　fragrant sakura mochi
　　　Gravity winning

Aggression

Being colorful
morning glories advertise
Hummingbirds love red

Fur

Black cat in the street
smart tabby out back napping
Dogs on the SWAT team

Overhead
  Birds pursuing bugs
  ten thousand a living wave
  Albatross aloft

5:00 AM
    White brown black yellow
    flowering Americans
    Night blooming assholes

Waiting
There's more oxygen
in those cold northern waters.
Smart white ice hunters

7:00 AM

Mona Lisa smile

good morning America

Ipomoea

Cachet

Lapis lazuli
Michelangelo's ceiling
Monet's poppy red

Logic

Volcanos erupt
avalanches know no names
Eggs by the trillions

Sons

Protective at first
the paternal cannibal.
Envy emerging

Imperatives

She everywhere
breeds lives so cheap, flies birds sheep
Spring after winter

Entubation

The Pope overnight
death is in the hands of God
Plop goes the old frog

New Yorkers
    Streets, gray concrete dust
    twisted steel, glass, shattered dreams.
    Craving Krispy Kremes

Incoming

Lava, crashing stones
time orchestrating great crimes.
Some old cats can spray

Crystallizing
   Pursuing phantoms
   speculating on thin ice
   Gravity and light

Aristotle

Timeless tireless mind
circling a favorite stick
Crabs crossing the beach

Return to Tsugaru
    Personal moments
    allowing for perfection
    Drink yourself purple

The Setting Sun
Forever shaping
father and son then no one
In particular

No Longer Human
  You let it go by
  the undrunk glass of absinthe
  This lonely winter

Oda's Web

Water polished stones
green dust on a summer wind
Suddenly a web

Absinthe
        Wormwood, angelica
        hyssop, anise, licorice
        Not so Ordinaire

LA

Avoiding oneanother
cars cars cars cars cars more cars
Buying a sun tan

San Francisco
  Is there any pride
  bent-over naked butts here there?
  Hunting cigarettes

Forever
    Driven, passionate
    poet, artist, musician
    Poppies are da kind

Good Morning
Devil wearing fur
fuzz all over everything
Window silhouette

Hittites

Fabulous brick domes
black cobras, purple eggplants
Underground cities

Time

Longtime coming...home
Golden Gate Bridge coyotes
Crows cruisin' for fries

Tokyo Wave

Bright gray, umbrellas
men, women, kids, bikes, no dogs
Rain Tree coffee lounge

Shinjuki
Arcs of perfection
unearthly edges, white cloth
Van Gogh's Sunflowers

Rainbows

Sandy Hanalei
walking on water with friends
Never too many

Santa Fe
What art gallery
indians selling silver
Cool blue mountain air

Lima

A verdant garden
colonial perfection
The snow queen died young

Cuzco

Heart on a skewer
water cannon threatening
Her coca-drool smile

Machu-Picchu
Thin air high up there
their silver now new world gold
Coca leaf dreaming

Hecho en Mexico

Long ago up on top
the Pyramid of the Sun.
Dyed green stone fading

Galapagos
    Iridescent shoals
    frigate birds, island finches.
    Darwin knew pigeons

Santa Cruz Island
Darwin's finch atop
the nonchalant iguana.
No poets complaining

Kyoto River Walk
    Taking a whole day
    to buy the tiny metal pipe
    Save me, Oh! Save me

Clubbing
The Revolution
Carnaby brawls, Woodstock mud
Nineteen sixty-nine

Afghanistan

Old sandstone buddha
calls to prayer, singing quail.
Want chicken? grab one!

Pakistan
        Most rent their clothes
        the few own everything
        Great creme caramel

Tourists

El Prado Goya
Velásquez, Brueghel, Dürer
What about Madrid?

Strings

Three Michelin stars
Luxembourg Garden puppets
Who can remember?

South of Naples
  Shotgun, sport jacket
  plowing with an ancient mule.
  Real local color

544 AD
Tea of Bamiyan
rhodiola rosea
3rd eye of Buddha

Polar Landing
Life in outer space
aliens moving around
Needy cat today

Perception
    Dust balls floating by
a curious distraction.
The untroubled mind

Red Eye
Birds come to see her
listening from the bird bath.
Cats personalize

1000 Full Moons
   Cycles adding up
   seven eleven thirteen.
   Poet's checkout line

Rumi

We are what we try
history entwines in time.
Tall wisteria

Change
What will it become
that one outgrowing its pot
Body Mass Index

Acapulco Sunburn

Too much fun snorkeling
fishing for sharks with a Ford
Fruit bowl centipede

Nose

Ryoanji flash back
OH! That incense takes me there
Coffee...tobacco

Color Blind

Green trees green money
got to love that green power
Whithering forests

SUV

Gasoline ice cream
already too fat for cars
Passenger pigeons

Whiteous
        Evangelicals
    oh so proud to be all white
    Old World goldenrod

Sambo Santa
   Holiday turkey
   Japan inhales and exhales
   Chocolate mochi

Society of Spectacle
Post modernity
just buy me for what I am
Where is my red dot?

One Day
Energy crisis
electric rabbits can't run
Dog races cancelled

Eternity
 Always the unknown
 hard to see...so hard to know
 Ad infinitum

Words

Language has many
available dimensions
Four fingers one thumb

Searching
　　　Walkabout looking
　　　a thousand miles of Paris
　　　Darkness before dawn

Work
  Your reality
    your own to rationalize
    Surf and fish make sand

Aging

How dark must it be
to see the important stars
Sitting pink in time

Safe Sex
No one's having sex
when eating for two people
Gasoline ice cream

Ripley's
Believe it or not
we have a perfect teacher
Watch television

Favorites

Potatoes, gravy
fried chicken, corn, black pepper
Chicken before egg

Really
   Just look at those eyes
   warm chicken soup and crunchies
   Cats do feel more self

Tea 5G
Five grams of matcha
four tablespoons of sugar
Two cups of water

The Forest

The darkness looming
in the art world old and new
Look how tall he is!

Lin Yutang
Tasteless, odorless
colorless, expensive, so
Perfectly Chinese

Pretty Color

Redwood decks, hot tubs
California's finest
A feast all but gone

Mosquitos

Oil well heads down up
down sucking up down sucking
California

Sun-warm Sand
Famous wildflowers
birds, bees, males, females, sunshine
Basho's bananas

Devil's Slide

Gray whales on sandbars
crunching pesky barnacles
Crows fly by for fries

Release
Food in abundance
competition New York style
Rain forest night noise

Stuck

Those names stuck in time
starlight and moonshine and fame
In purgatory

1938

Ergot, hydroxide
lithium, amine, tartrate
How the truth is found

Sirens

Teepee wikiup
new ways not always enough
Modern tornados

Gifu

Light, dark raku bowl
fine old white kiri wood box
Foamy green sencha

Sensations
   Electricity
   coffee, tea, morning glory
   On the phone...just words

Pheromones

Roses, datura
fragrant white chrysanthemums
Red ants, black ants, bees

Horizons
   Ipomoea
   amanita, datura
   Tracks of little deer

Nihonga

Atmospheric, thick
musty moody centuries
Pungent horse radish

Agendas
    Beauty no concern
    fly on the wall nonchalant
    Sakura mochi

Paying Attention

Perfect tea weather
spring clouds becoming summer
Between ideas

Old Metate
   Black women pounding
   history stolen away
   Cat's favorite bowl

Cobwebs

Old dirt is better
they don't make it like before
Peyote gasping

Vagabondage
   Alive, girls, sunshine
   complain to God about the rain
   Rivers of red wine

Togetherness

Gasoline ice cream
holidays, the good ole daze
Air traffic control

Don't Won't Can't
   The empty wrapper
Milky Way Dark OMG
Absinthe untasted

Nightly
　Engorged sensations
　undulating pulsing pairs
　Stories told by stars

Nose

Sensualist knows
garlic booze tobacco pot
High Sierra pine

Liberty really
Men came and mixed in
women came and sorted out
Cattle here sheep there

Daze

Nebulous jungle
a blither of famous names
Who lives in LA?

Cordova
Pirate skulls and bones
architecture to die for
No salt in the bread

de los Caballeros
Old brown stone walled church
Teresa de Ávila
Wild boar for dinner

Seville

Dried blood on bone, whose?
a small splinter from which cross
Worth their weight in gold

Pink White

She dusts their green skin
the cats and birds watch for her
Peyote flowers

Who's There
Angels on a vine
or is that a baboon face
Ipomoea

Morning Noon Night
Bougainvillea
morning glory butterflies
Night blooming jasmine

Nature Provides
   Rain water soaked grain
   bubbling ecstatically
   Perfect Moon viewing

Floating World
    Yeast die happily
    conjuring the great spirits
    Whiskey, wine and beer

Choices
   Manhattan stories
   New Mexico cottonwoods
   Three million footsteps

Shopping
This side felt the sun
tapping the summer melon
Slippery with dew

Today
  Friends in high places
  Tokyo left Kyoto right
  Gifu bridge coin toss

Playing
   Gods bring home devils
   cats tormenting frightened mice
   Earth circling through time

Torrential
Water everywhere
old man river everywhere
Not a drop to drink

Oh Boy
Nightmarish cuckoo
waking neighbors too early
Moon viewing last night

Cruise Control

Eyes and inner ears
hallucinatory light
Ikebana spike

Kabuki cho
   Tenzaru soba
   short an important finger
   Sumo on TV

Fertile Crescent
Prozac patriots
all American Neros
The poppy provides

Aliens

If anywhere else
certainly here already
Milky Way freeway

Bingo

A blink of the eye
becoming yours forever
Ummm...hot cinnamon

Important
Unique in the world
fresh kuri-manju robot
Ueno Station

Perfect Cafes
    Get up, get going
    morning coffee and sugar
    Hummingbird heaven

Vitamin D
Morning butterfly
today white on white jasmine
The heat of the sun

Interstellar
Aliens maybe
extraterrestrial gold
Active here and now

Old Antwerp
   The Golden Compasses
   the Bible never the same
   Perfect espalier

Awareness

Sea bass, pork, chicken
the cat has preferences
Fresh from the best stores

Why

Green is green not brown
but Chinese green tea is brown
Red lead great for toys

Talent

Life flowing through air
timing always an essence
Having heard that voice

Seasonally
  The cast fly snakes out
  falling in...the rainbow strikes
  Today a barbed hook

Tako Dozo
  Water ankle deep
  colorful hunger around
  White moray tonight

After Eden
Always the gambler
buying in adding some time
Today planting rice

Zen When

Gate closed already
the Leica makes it open
Bishop's tea party

Tenerife
Anchors dragged up
gobs of oil down on the sand
Angry southwest wind

Cafe Dreamin'
Roasting salted words
a grove of exotic nuts
Poems by poets

You
        White out or bleed out
        or black out or gray away
        The Revelation

Red Eye

Their spot is better
over there look at that one
Look what they're getting

Using the Light

Rabbits are springtime
parrots quite like all of us
Candles meant to burn

Again

Shadow of the hawk
ants trapped in leaking honey
Cat on the duvet

Body English

Rowing on water
wind sky currents the colors
Backing into life

Save Me SAVE ME
Keen apprehension
empowering all feeling
Pure desperation

Rikyu

Just the right water
just the right old raku bowl
Just the right green tea

Seami

Start in the middle
maybe climb a few tall trees
Daily life mostly

Picasso

Primitive juju
coloring appearances
Blue water lily

Escher

Metamorphosis
snakes swans people black and white
Magic in black light

O'Keeffe
New York City women
carefully arranged flowers
Abiquiu cross bones

Eye Candy
Bright stars big colors
recognizability
The electric chair

Cinnamon
Your man of the Moon
promising sweet tomorrows
Fragrant morning air

Yawn

Something he might eat
the cat watched it walking home
The faraway man

July

Jacaranda wow
lilac immediately
Now and then again

Sunshine
   Civil rights white light
   caterpillars who ask who
   White rabbits fleeing

Monarchy
A flying feather
yellow then white now yellow
Traveling through time

In Cars

Oysters in tight shells
alone in splendid armour
Coming and going

Bruce Lee
The fat ones swagger
toes out always belly first
Potato can't twist

Kyoto Maples
　　Sky lace of spring leaves
　　here in the Korean stone
　　Water and bamboo

Nara

So much for so long
red deer bowing politely
Portal to Heaven

Kyōsai

Ant line of ideas
poets sumi patrons wine
Going with the flow

Early Fragrances
  Conceiving zero
  steel dharma saffon yellow
  Tears of the Buddha

Dancing Together
 Bird bath near a wall
 reflecting everything
 Bright silent music

Aspen

Ten thousand and more
suns shine bright every night
Old Sol makes our day

Gravitation

Seeking completion
dirt gathering on the ground
Sun melting butter

Gravity
 Intentions in line

  connecting days and nights
  The cat will want food

Biennial Bubbles
By any at all
what a fabulous tulip!
Buy all at any

ATCG
   Exhale inhale air
   inhale exhale inhale...breathe
   Birds fish we they trees

Pizzaz

Plum blossom spear blur
emeralds diamonds pearls
Sundews flytraps lunch

Michelangelo
Carrara morning
dark river half white with dust
David more than stone

Straight Up
   Uncoiling smoothly
   Wisteria and the Sun
   Lavender cascade

Linear

Earth Moon Sun circling
morning glory wants to climb
People seek straight lines

Walking
    Every morning
    looking forward to seeing
    The warmth of the Sun

Cafes

Every morning
anticipating feeling
The warmth of a friend

Curious

Ask the old tree there
why are battles fought here?
Squirrels love walnuts

Communications

    He loves fried chicken

    cat on a banana leaf

    A way without words

Be Like
   Who picks up pennies
   who never picks up any
   The cats see it all

Honk
Cabinet redux
deSuburbanization
Geese in the schoolyard

JuJu Mana JuJu
What's in a TIKI
a lizard older than you
Ipomoea

Guzzle

Basho in New York
dancing at a TIKI bar
Plop! goes the old frog

Sprawl

Which way freeway signs
eighty miles east of SF
Yosemite WOW!

Morning
Well-worn kimono
welcome cherry blossoms ya
Sand path freshly raked

Change

Exceptionalism

Michigan tart cherry pie

Passenger pigeons

Being

No birds watch for me

crows and doves wait for Sally

refreshing bird bath

Mainstream

Ball for all that's all
laser leveled plastic grass
OMG endplay!

1962

Cruel wind broke the limb

offering perfect apples

Mushrooms in the Sun!

North Beach

The withering wail

wannabe alcoholics

Once-was neighborhood

Truth

Color designed for

tan ro ku bon moodiness

Versimilatude

TikTok

Life's wasted mornings
left in empty wine bottles
Suddenly it's dusk

Always

Bright avant-garde light
in the darkness before dawn
Easy to see later

Creativity

Meditation with

a cat in the studio

Being quiet rain

Devil's Slide

Tipped and tilted
in just the place to share
Acapulco Gold!

Celebrity

Ahh! Their approval...
nothing like people clapping
Strangers who need me!

Artists

Challenging beauty

with the fine art of being

Only poetry

Smooth

The thoughtful zen monk
grooms the old trees before lunch
And enlightenment

September 2021

Bright orange outside

fluttering shadows inside

Monarchs migrating

Dr. Ordinaire

Wormwood Melissa

Hissop Anise Everclear

Absinthe martini!

Another

Holiday dinners

everyone all at once

I heard so they say

Winter

So many seasons
looking into the forest
Myo like yugen

Decades

Cycle of seasons

dark obscure enlightenments

Myo like yugen

Conceptualism

Fevered imaginings
exhaled into public space
Rainbows in the chill

Legacy

No Chinese pheasants
in Waldseemueller's new world
Coming soon: Fry Bread

Somniferum

Seeds sprinkled on snow
soon spring into summer pods
Colorfully white!

Tall

Inhale to sooth need

trees center themselves or fall

Sudden summer gale!

The Croz

The little devils

who come to us as angels

Come and go you know

Zip Code

You are where you live

just as you are what you eat

Becoming your street

Avante-garde

Keyboard color space
the game gambits and players
No damage no truth

Bingo!

Ahh so zen again

breathing summer in and out

Eye-high white poppies!

Lookin' back

    Livin' and smokin'

    Leaves of Grass nice flowers too

    Music of the Spheres

Dawn

Twittering outside
life, a gift of the mother
Spring green unfolding

Success

U S A today
Red White and Blue, SUGAR TOO
Body Mass Index

kerCHOO!
Craving live oysters
onanism in words and needs
Golden rod pollen

Family
Mom dad grand-parents
brother sister son daughter.
People on a bus

Gardening

Monks raking away
becoming a zen garden
Woodpeckers beyond

WOKE

Singing birds woke me
cherry trees bright with blossoms
Sakura mochi

Hungry!
  Impatience rushes
  wind before a coming storm
  Downstream trout waiting

Full Share

Shadow vanishing
black cat passing silently
One thousand full moons

Vampira
    Leaves of Grass intone
    drama homosensual
    Kissing dying boys

Business

We are what hands do
so few transcend Chakra two
Monkeys exploring

Yosemite

There on a high rock
imagine the aroma
A distant campfire

Fuzzy

They wear fancy fur
surviving by distracting
Sartorial cats

Everywhere
    Small, ordinary
    yet seen by impatient eyes
    Alley cat jumping

After Coffee
Three seed sourdough
french toast with maple syrup
Extraordinaire

Noon

Bagel with goat cheese
half a red Envy apple
Double espresso

Appetizing
   Dashi, soy, mirin
   tofu, clear noodles, cabbage
   Sukiyaki bowls

Clarity

Roses not so red
myriad leaves not so green
Other eyes at night

Tails

Fur-on-fur cats find
soft touch worth a thousand words
Wind strumming bamboo

Mornings

Dark morning mirrors
the dawn colors upside down
Rain sweetened the air

Ubiquity
A sip opens doors
any more beckons devils
Dandelion wine

Tokyo
Crows bigger than cats
cats bigger than ancient trees
Beer vending machines

Beaches

Gray sea bird feathers
surf smashed crabs and jellyfish
Golden kelp black flies

Beyond
    Continuing routines
    time trumps talent, ways and means
    Ipomoea

Art

Sublime quintessence
Routine and tragedy
Morning glory white

Auspicious

Call it a rain dance
call it a fine art opening
Showers make it grow

Smelly

I'm a cat, that's that
forget surf. What's for dinner?
Smell of sea wet suits

Solutions

The latest science
select facts freshly shaken
Today's recipe

Reality
The cat seems healthy
likes eating off of the ground
Hetch Hetchy water

Gonnabe

Throwing fancy darts
at the Moon time and again
Last seen in a bar

Oh My!
Longing for release
simplicity of orgasm
Dawn of a new day

Yeah

Human potential
finding pleasure on a wave
Dawn of a new day

Big Small
Charisma a sum
factor in avoirdupois
more becoming less

Noon Again

All night gulping booze
all morning gulping water
The place needs cleaning

Yummy

My Milky Way Dark
preferred sugar of the gods
Hummingbirds love red

Age

Silent wall of stone
pretty pebbles chattering
Ipomoea

Huh?

If you want to know
what's happening in your life
Ask your neighbor's cat

Oh No
Another hairball
born with fur and lots of it
To annoy humans

Cycling

New years come quickly
yesterdays birds here today
Making new paintings

Amerika
Looking for Basho
who do we get? Walt Whitman
Dandelion wine

Owe

Ode to poetry
there's no fucking life support
Feral cats die young

Passing
    Earthly enchantments
    Leaves of Grass to save your ass
    Sweetness of flowers

Tradition

Long pig logic holds
the more people the more food
Worms make the garden

Colors

Brown is red and green
Brown is not like black and white
Color all its own

Redux

Who would imagine
Basho in America
Frogs and bananas

Everyone
 Following the stars
 night after night after night
 Pollen on old dust

Early
Fresh air clean water
people looking for coffee
Dawn of a new day

Daze

Up early pink sky
Happy Donuts hot coffee
Suddenly dinner

Perpetual
  The elegant brush
  four dimensions become two
  Lightning fills the eye!

Circuit

What's in a painting?
circuits to capture lightning
Fireflies in a jar

MFA

Money For Artists
Mother's Favorite Artist
More Fucking Artists

Nihonga
Classic iris pond
a low stone wall to enjoy
Vigilant koi

Snappy
Sticky prose enough?
tickling curiosity.
Cat nails big fat rat

Design

First cherry blossoms
soon sakura leaf mochi
Green tea over rice.

Enku

Nata-bori ka

Hatchet finding the Buddha

Wearing green cypress

See

Rapa Nui tall
giant old stone Maoi
Watching out to sea

Kireji

Keri ramu ka

tsu ya ramu ran kana

Nifty spider's web

Walk About
       Serendipity
       star bursts of fragrant flavor
       Roadside strawberries

Nikko

One thousand steps ha
see no hear no say no ya
Over Shinkyo Bridge

Bone

Crows love their food soft
water appreciated
Gift left at deck door

Among
   Walking tinker toys
   alcoholic wannabes
   North Beach then and now

Observed

Animals don't read books
mapping terroir sniff by sniff
Peyote woman

Nata-Bori

Seeking the Buddha
Tree in mind hatchet in hand
Sakura mochi

Baishinshi

Scrying with a knife
kogatane wicked sharp
So easy to bleed!

Typical
AH! an idea
which another puts to words.
Someone else gets paid

Ordinary
    Americans teach
    White cowboys – red indians.
    Turtles on a log

Ummm!
Love that saute pan
olive oil and whatever
Garlic always works

Moonshine

Seventy seven
a lifetime of blue light nights
One thousand full Moons

Belief
Jesus came and went
Luther, Boorhaus, Smith, Darwin
Raccoons rattling cans

Shape

Rhetorical WHAT!
Seasonal color WHERE WHEN.
Conceptual WHY?

Bread
Delicious excess
life...a gift of the mother
Solar empowered.

Alive

Chicken first? Egg first?
life, a gift of the mother
Spring puffing pollen

Pods

Seeds enough and more
all tomorrows reassured
Pollen aplenty

Updraft
Acrobatic crows
zoom beach scouring for french fries.
Potato patch sharks

Sloat

White water roiling
Earth Moon dancing with the Stars
Tiny grains of sand

Curiosities

Born ready to go
hitch-hiking not an option
Trekking the Wakhan

Cosmos

Moon-glow demigod
invisible without Sun.
Seed pods trump the odds

Girl Street Kyoto
  Me...the bicyclist
  My Way! Get out of My Way!
  Running of the bulls

Bernal Hilltop

Red tail hawk watching

the impatient gopher soon

Breakfast lunch dinner

Chromosomal
   Grabby: that I am
   and given...being human.
   Cats having kittens

Backyard Bard

Lisbon Lemon tree
a glorious poet indeed!
Born green...ripening

Earthlings

Son of Sam Cherry
yearning for celebrity
A short Oscar Wilde

Accolade

One thousand poems
a million hopeful moments
WOW! Listen! Clapping

Ultraviolet

    Hummingbirds searching
    ephemeral red flowers
    Sun always on time

Hidden

GONG!

Dark perilous cliff
as ever, preoccupied
Butterfly dreaming

Drama

The whole envisioned
music costume dialogue
Seami...Shakespeare

Me-Me

Tinker toy bad boys
poet's way or the highway
Fast...shallow water

American Pie
  Brown-headed cowbirds
  buffalo soldiers thieving
  Indian outrage

Wannabe

Gobbling without looking
raisins proving to be flies
Blind poets grasping

OB whispering
    Happy cat cooing
    birds do it, humans need it
    Sound of sea water

Fifty years
Neeli Cherkovski
thoughtful friends hard to come by
A favorite beach

Penumbra

The lucky die young
others left to close the door
Ask any mushroom

Giving back
　　Life, ten million breaths
　　inhaling...exhaling each
　　At times a poem

Naturally

Green back then green now
bits and pieces sweet salty sour
Tokyo street trees

Knock Knock
Hello! anyone home?
limbo...is this Heaven's door?
Old Mortality

Andover Noon

Yet another coffee
Table of so many dreams
Poet Laureate?

Me

One year plus one day
Alamogordo BIG BANG!
The old frog goes plop.

You

Two weeks plus one day
Alamogordo BIG BANG!
The old frog goes plop.

Remember
Myriad green leaves
yellow becoming purple
Omly one so red

Fated

Neeli Cherkovski
wannabe gannabe ghost
Born Nelson Cherry

Buzz

Bernal dog walkers
beatnik poet in the news
The empty porch chair

Magritte
  Those white wings, block dots
on dandelion yellow
  Poet butterfly

Ghosts

Round porch table waits
empty chair forever quiet
Barking at shadows

Bluebird
 What's the big worry?
 flown-away budgie came home,
 Oysters live with pearls

Rendezvous

Coffee way back when
Caffe Trieste dreamers GONG!
Social butterfly

Sally Out

Broken clouds...blue sky
Sun warming empty table.
Walking Neeli's dog

Made in United States
Troutdale, OR
06/13/2024

20513751R10190